ICKY WORLD

WE NEED FUNGUS!

By Addy Farmer
Illustrated by Scott Garrett

Gareth Stevens
PUBLISHING

Please visit our website, www.garethstevens.com. For a free color catalog of all our high-quality books, call toll free 1-800-542-2595 or fax 1-877-542-2596.

Cataloging-in-Publication Data
Names: Farmer, Addy. | Garrett, Scott.
Title: We need fungus! / Addy Farmer, illustrated by Scott Garrett.
Description: Buffalo, NY : Gareth Stevens Publishing, 2026. | Series: Icky world | Includes glossary and index.
Identifiers: ISBN 9781482472943 (pbk.) | ISBN 9781482472950 (library bound) | ISBN 9781482472967 (ebook)
Subjects: LCSH: Fungi--Juvenile literature.

Clasification: LCC QK603.5 F376 2026 | DDC 579.5--dc23

Published in 2026 by
Gareth Stevens Publishing
2544 Clinton St.
Buffalo, NY 14224

First published in Great Britain in 2023 by Wayland
Copyright © Hodder and Stoughton, 2023

Series Editor: Grace Glendinning
Series Designer: Peter Scoulding

The website addresses (URLs) included in this book were valid at the time of going to press. However, it is possible that contents or addresses may have changed since the publication of this book. No responsibility for any such changes can be accepted by either the author or the Publisher.

All rights reserved. No part of this book may be reproduced in any form without permission in writing from the publisher, except by a reviewer.

Printed in the United States of America

CPSIA compliance information: Batch #CSGS26: For further information contact Gareth Stevens at 1-800-542-2595.

Find us on

CONTENTS

What on Earth is fungus?	4
In the beginning ... there was fungus!	6
How does a fungus live and grow?	8
Fungi and insects	10
Lichens: a special partnership	12
Woodland wonders	14
Wood-wide web	16
Fungi extreme!	18
The inspiration of fungus	20
Fungi: wonder medicine?	22
Fungi as food and food for thought	24
Fungi can save our world!	26
What you can do for a fungus near you	28
Glossary	30
Further info	31
Index	32

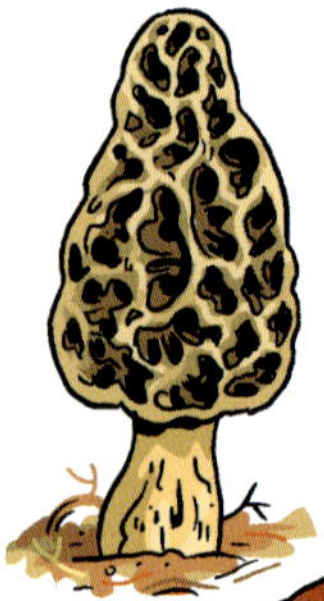

What on Earth is fungus?

A fungus is an organism that is neither a plant nor an animal. When there is more than one fungus, they are called fungi.

Millions of fungi

It's not just mushrooms and toadstools! There are lots of other fungi, such as molds, mildews, plant rusts, lichens, and yeasts.

Mycologists (fungi scientists) think that there are at least 3 to 4 million different species of fungi.

Fungi are found everywhere on Earth, from the bottom of the oceans to inside you, from the single-celled bread yeast fungus, which makes bread rise, to the world's largest organism, the humongous honey fungus.

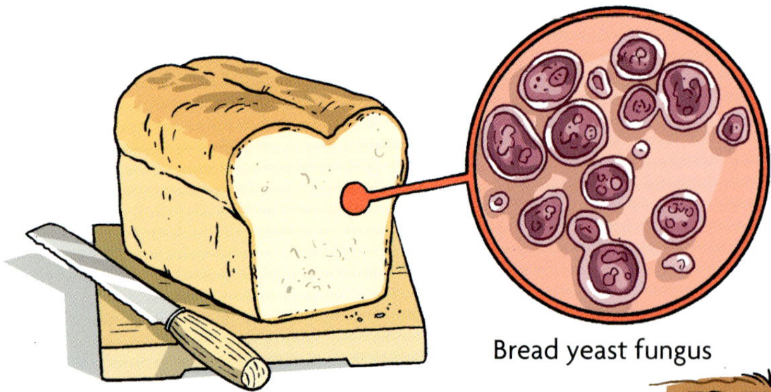

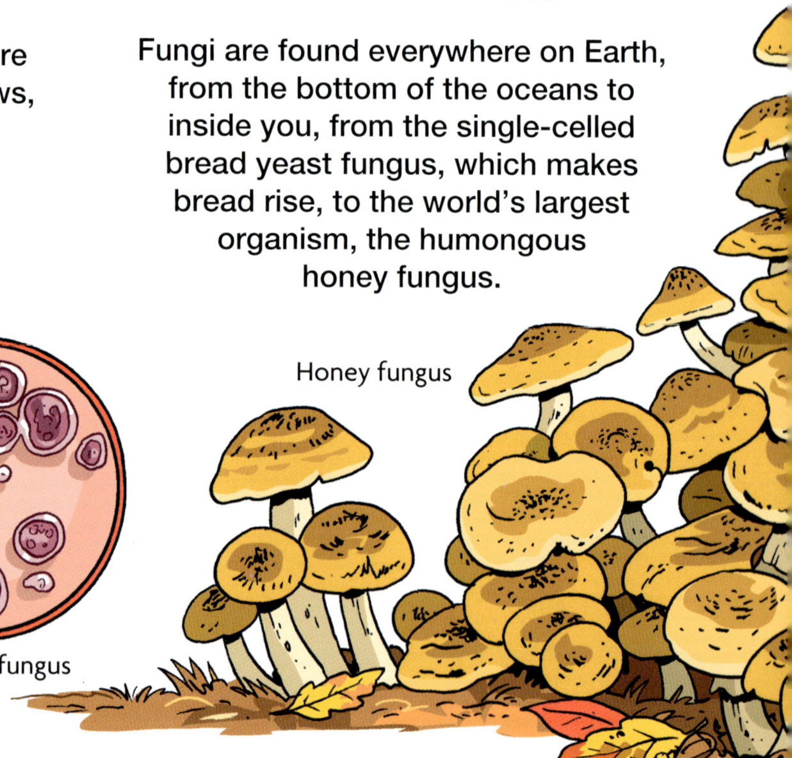

Most of the fungus is underground in microscopic threads, which make up a mycelium.

Fungi working hard

In this book, we'll see how fungi are nature's recyclers and do the vital job of decomposing. Without fungi, the world would be smothered in dead plants and animals!

Bracket fungi

Fantastic fungi!

Humans have made use of fungi for thousands of years and for many different purposes, from food to medicine.

We'll learn about the fungi you can see and the vast network of fungi hidden underground.

It's truly amazing how fungi survive and thrive by teaming up with, or taking over, other plants and animals.

Fungi are everywhere and they always have been ...

In the beginning ... there was fungus!

Fungi have been on Earth for billions of years and may even have helped to develop the first life on Earth. They do not have brains, but they have always worked out how to find food, reproduce, and grow.

First life from fungi?

Some scientists suggest that microscopic fungi may have helped Earth's first plants–algae–survive on land. This prehistoric algae may have piggybacked on fungi to leave the water for the first time, over 500 million years ago.

It is thought that fungi helped these early plants, which did not yet have proper roots, to take up nutrients from the ground. Gradually, the plants would take root, spreading across the Earth as land plants.

Fungal survivors

When an asteroid hit prehistoric Earth, it wiped out the dinosaurs and lots of plants. But fungi were there to help rebuild the world.

Ancient fungi could even find nutrients from minerals in rocks. When this happened, the rocks were very slowly turned into soil, giving plants a place to live and providing more nutrients.

Fungi as ecosystem engineers

Underground, the fungal mycelium formed a network surrounding the plant roots, called mycorrhiza. This network helped keep the soil stable so that plants could send their roots deep into the soil and hold firm.

How does a fungus live and grow?

Fantastic fungi can absorb nutrients from whatever they are living on or in. That includes humans and other animals!

Team fungi

Today, microscopic fungi still live inside most of Earth's plants. Protecting each other, exchanging nutrients, and even fighting each other. This is called symbiosis.

Microscopic fungi also live in the guts and mouths of animals, including humans. They help us digest food and battle some invaders.

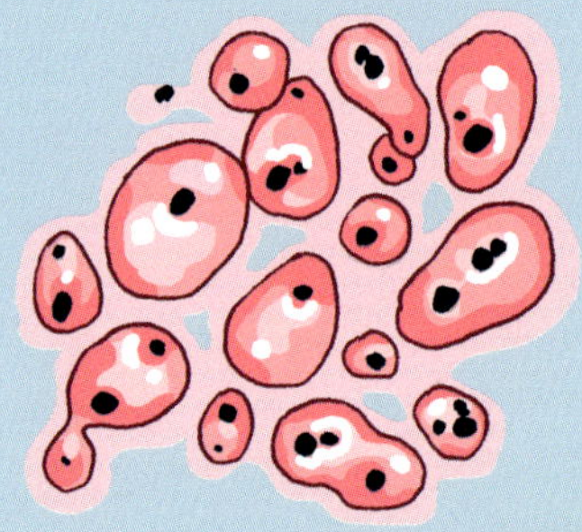

Human mouth fungus

Human gut fungus

Athlete's foot fungus

Parasitic fungi

There are also fungi that feed off *unwilling* hosts. An example of this is athlete's foot, which is a fungus that feeds on keratin in the dead skin between your toes. Smart, but itchy!

How fungus spreads

A fungus usually reproduces by forming and releasing spores.

When a giant puffball mushroom pops it can send out 7 trillion spores!

Some spores will be blown by the wind and rain, but some might hitch a ride on a passing animal.

Some fungi have developed special scents to attract spore-spreaders. Flies love the smell of the stinkhorn mushroom, for example, and pick up spores as they land.

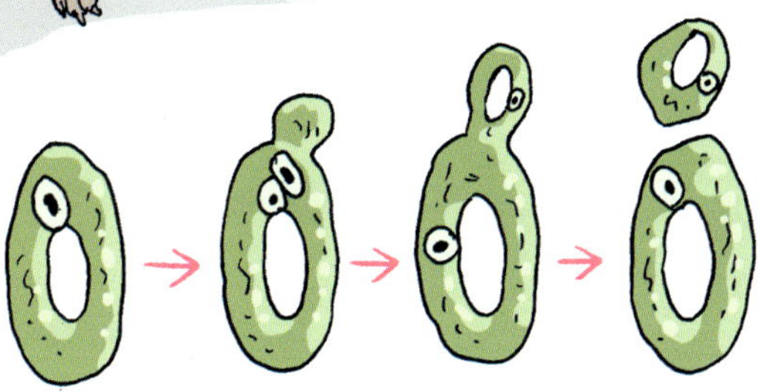

Some fungi don't need buddies

Baker's yeast is a fungus that grows by budding instead of spreading spores. If there is food and water to energize it, this single-cell fungi will split in half again and again all by itself!

Fungi and insects

Different types of fungi have some amazing partnerships with insects, which can be both good and bad for their hosts.

Fungi gardens

Beneath the rainforests of South America lives a fungus that decomposes around 50,000 leaves a day.

Leafcutter ants grow a garden of these fungi by bringing them fresh leaves to eat, protecting them, and tidying up around them.

In return, the fungus acts as a food source for the ants' larvae.

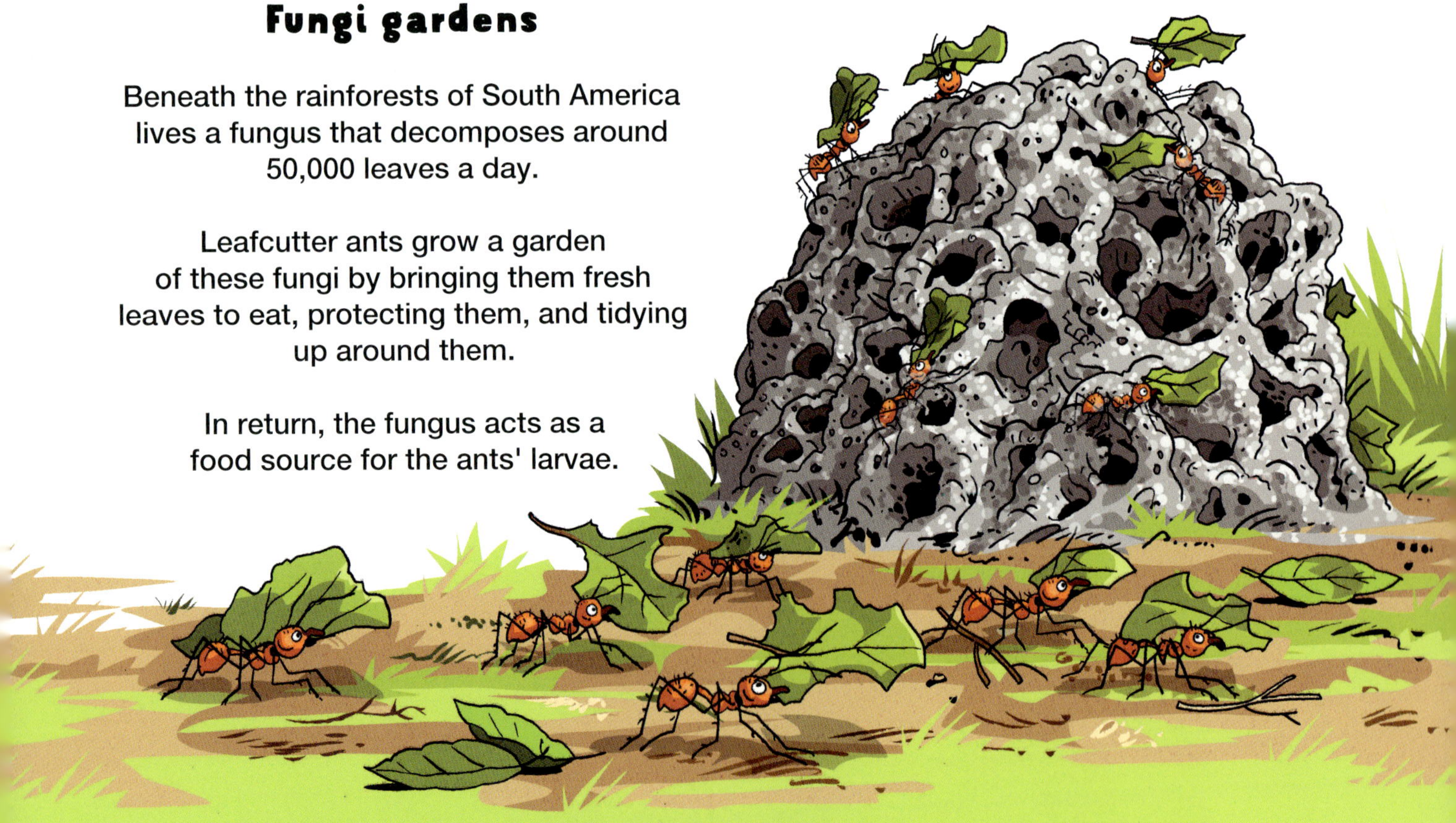

Sometimes it's hard to know who's the mastermind of these farming relationships: the fungus or the insect!

Multiuse fungi

Some termites also grow fungus gardens to feed their young inside their mounds.

The fungus also serves to decompose the termite poop and makes a compost that the termites then eat again. It's fungal recycling!

Zombie fungi?!

In tropical forests, the amazing zombie fungi feed on living insects and turn them into zombies. The fungus controls the insect's body from the inside.

The fungus forces the creature's legs to "walk" to a nice, high spot–a good place to spread spores.

Then the fungus pops out through the insect's head and its spores fly out, infecting many more insects in the ground!

Lichens: a special partnership

Lichens are fungi and algae working together. They come in a huge array of shapes and colors and are very important for ecosystems across the world.

Natural pioneers!

Lichens grow anywhere and everywhere: in water, on rocks, bark, soil, and even cars.

Lichens tell a pollution story

Lichens can survive in polluted areas, but they really thrive and spread in clean air.

Because of this, they are called "bioindicators," as they show us if an area has clean or polluted air.

We should all like lichens!

Lichens look after nature

In boreal forests, or found in the far north of Earth, lichen-cover protects trees and rocks from rain, wind, and snow.

If you go further north to the Arctic tundra, lichens replace trees entirely and are excellent at capturing carbon, a gas that is affecting global warming.

Some birds use lichens to camouflage their nests.

Lichens are a miniature ecosystem for even smaller creatures too, such as the microscopic tardigrade.

Tardigrade (also called a water bear or moss piglet)

And lichens are an essential food source for reindeer!

Woodland wonders

Fungi are part of the world's clean-up crew. Without them, our woodlands would be piled high with dead leaves and wood.

Dead wood decomposers

Most woodland fungi absorb their nutrients from dead wood and leaves.

As the fungi decompose all that wood, leaf litter, and even dead animals, they take the nutrients they need and release the rest into the soil.

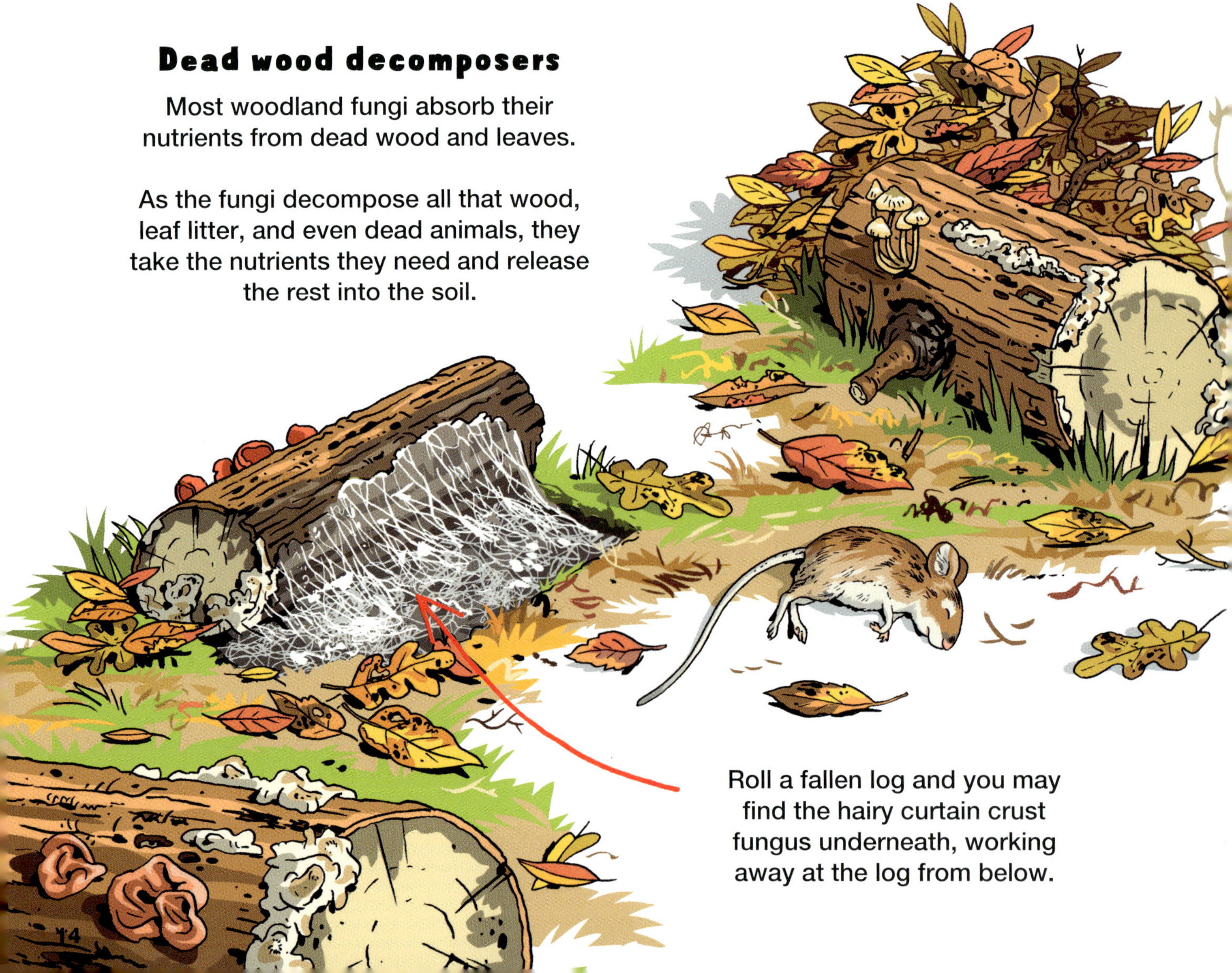

Roll a fallen log and you may find the hairy curtain crust fungus underneath, working away at the log from below.

Fungi with special skills

Wood is a tough material because it contains a compound called lignin, which is hard to break down.

"White-rot" was the first type of fungus ever to evolve the special skill of breaking down this tough part of a plant's cell–over 300 million years ago!

All these decomposer fungi clear the ground space for more plants to grow and help keep soil healthy.

*There are fungi that **destructively** consume living plants too, which is why a balanced ecosystem is so vital. Some parasitic fungi need to be kept in check!

Wood-wide web

Let's dig a bit deeper. There's a whole world beneath the surface ...

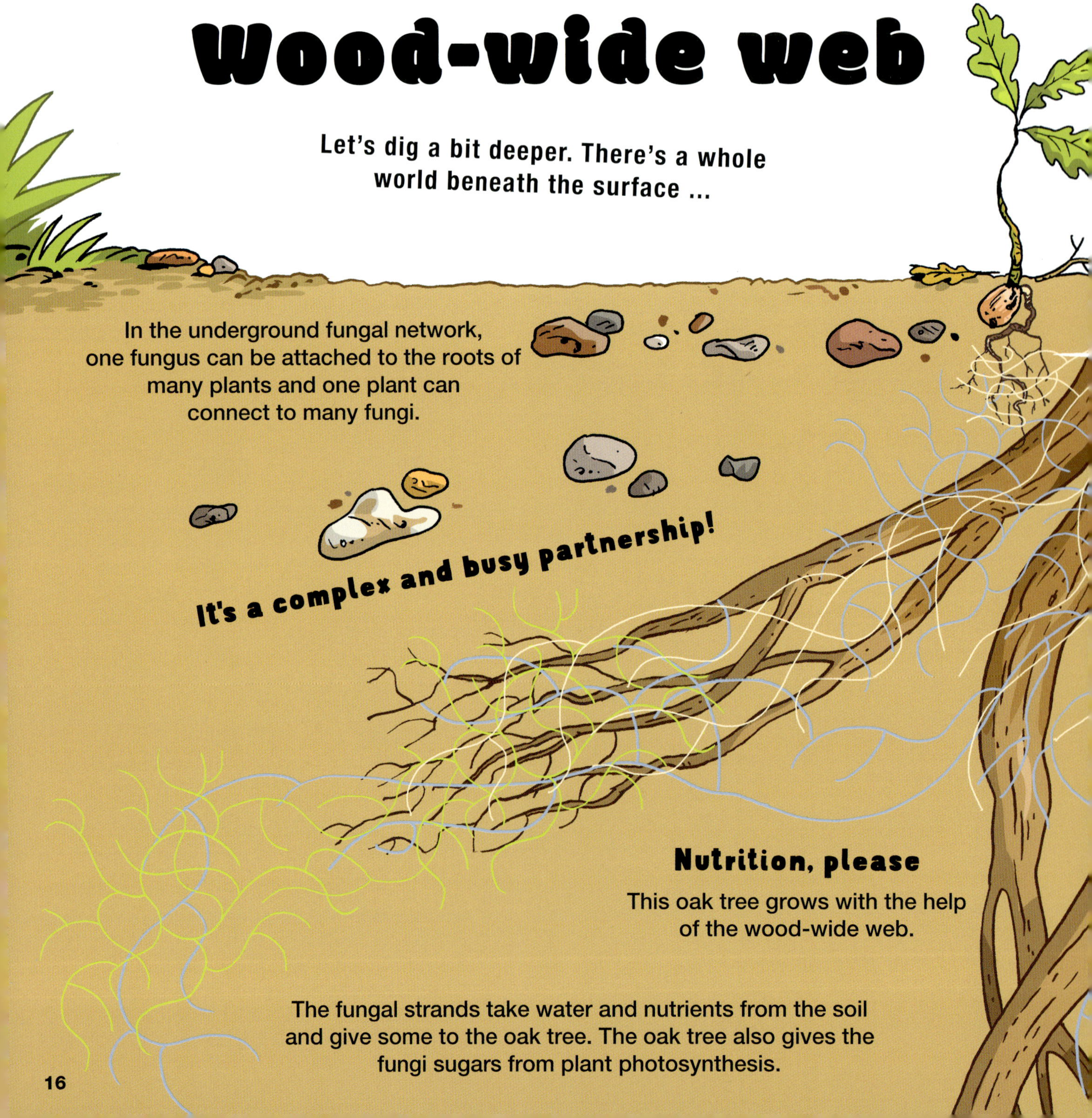

In the underground fungal network, one fungus can be attached to the roots of many plants and one plant can connect to many fungi.

It's a complex and busy partnership!

Nutrition, please

This oak tree grows with the help of the wood-wide web.

The fungal strands take water and nutrients from the soil and give some to the oak tree. The oak tree also gives the fungi sugars from plant photosynthesis.

Fungal information

With the help of the fungus web, trees can also connect to one another.

The mycorrhizal network delivers extra nourishment to the baby tree in the shade ...

... and sends the needed nutrients to the sick sapling.

Fungi help create a nutrient-rich, biodiverse and stable soil everywhere in the world.

This fungi and plant relationship has been going on for millions of years.

Fungi extreme!

From prehistory to today, we have seen how fungi can adapt and survive in all sorts of conditions. Here are some more extreme examples ...

Keeping sands stable

Mycorrhizal fungi are at work even in the sands of the desert, where there are few plants and very little water. They help to stop erosion, keeping the sands in place.

Fungi also form part of the "biocrust" or "living skin" of all deserts. This layer on top of the sand is key to the health of every living thing found in these extreme habitats.

Marine cleaners

Microscopic fungi at the bottom of the ocean help clean up dead matter, but might also be super-skilled at breaking down plastics and oil spills.

Scientists are working to see how we can use these pollution-busters to help with the huge amounts of micro-plastics in our oceans.

Fantastic black fungi

Black fungi are some of toughest fungi on Earth. They can live where almost nothing else can, such as the bare rock of the coldest valleys in the Antarctic.

Black fungi in the McMurdo Dry Valleys in Antarctica

In the area of the Chernobyl nuclear disaster, black fungi have been found to consume deadly radiation. As they do, they are helping to clean up this extremely polluted environment.

Black fungi: radiation-busters!

Fungus ... in space?

Fungi on the International Space Station were also observed absorbing the radiation on board. Astronauts may start using fungus shields!

Fungi can teach us a thing or two about cleaning up our environment (see how we can do more on pages 26–27) ...

The inspiration of fungus

People have often used the beauty and unique nature of fungi as inspiration for art and stories.

Enchanted mushrooms

Mushrooms grow so quickly that they seem to pop up out of nowhere. Their amazing growing skills have been explained through some interesting legends.

Beautiful fungi

The famous author Beatrix Potter wasn't just interested in naughty rabbits and frustrated farmers.

Years before she wrote children's books, like *The Tale of Peter Rabbit*, she studied fungi, especially lichens. Beatrix Potter was one of the earliest artists to study and draw mushrooms up close, and in their natural ecosystems.

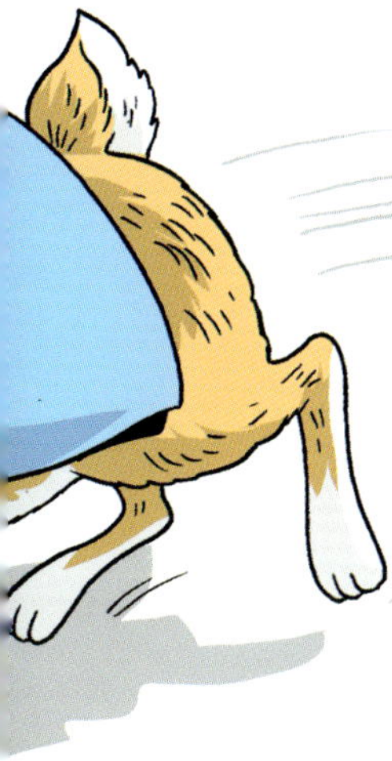

Reach out to fungi

The teamwork and resource-sharing of fungi can be an inspiration to humans.

Scientists and artists today understand that fungi live a fully connected life both above and below ground. Animals (including humans) and plants all benefit from fungal generosity!

Fungi: wonder medicine?

Fungi have been an important source of human medicine for thousands of years, through to today.

Bracket fungi

Caterpillar fungi

Fungi first aid

Early humans may have started it all. There is some evidence that they used bracket fungi as part of a first aid kit to help with all kinds of ailments.

Caterpillar fungi have also been used in some traditional medicines for centuries to treat ailments of the lungs, muscles, and kidneys.

Fleming and fungi

In 1928, the scientist Alexander Fleming came across a petri dish covered in a fungal mold. Instead of cleaning it up, he went on to harness its power as penicillin, the world's first "bacteria killer" or antibiotic.

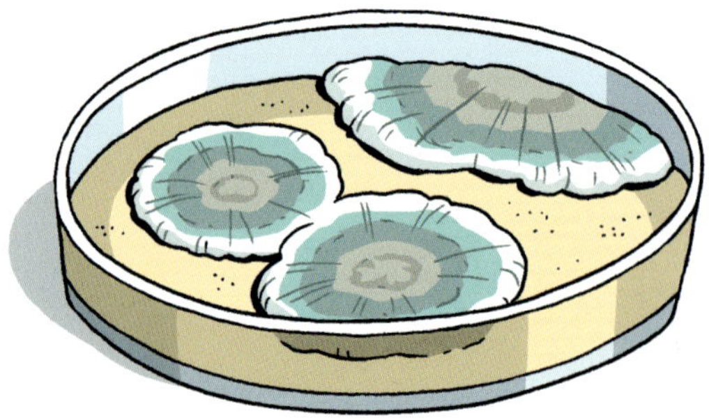

Petri dish

Antibiotics have gone on to change medicine forever!

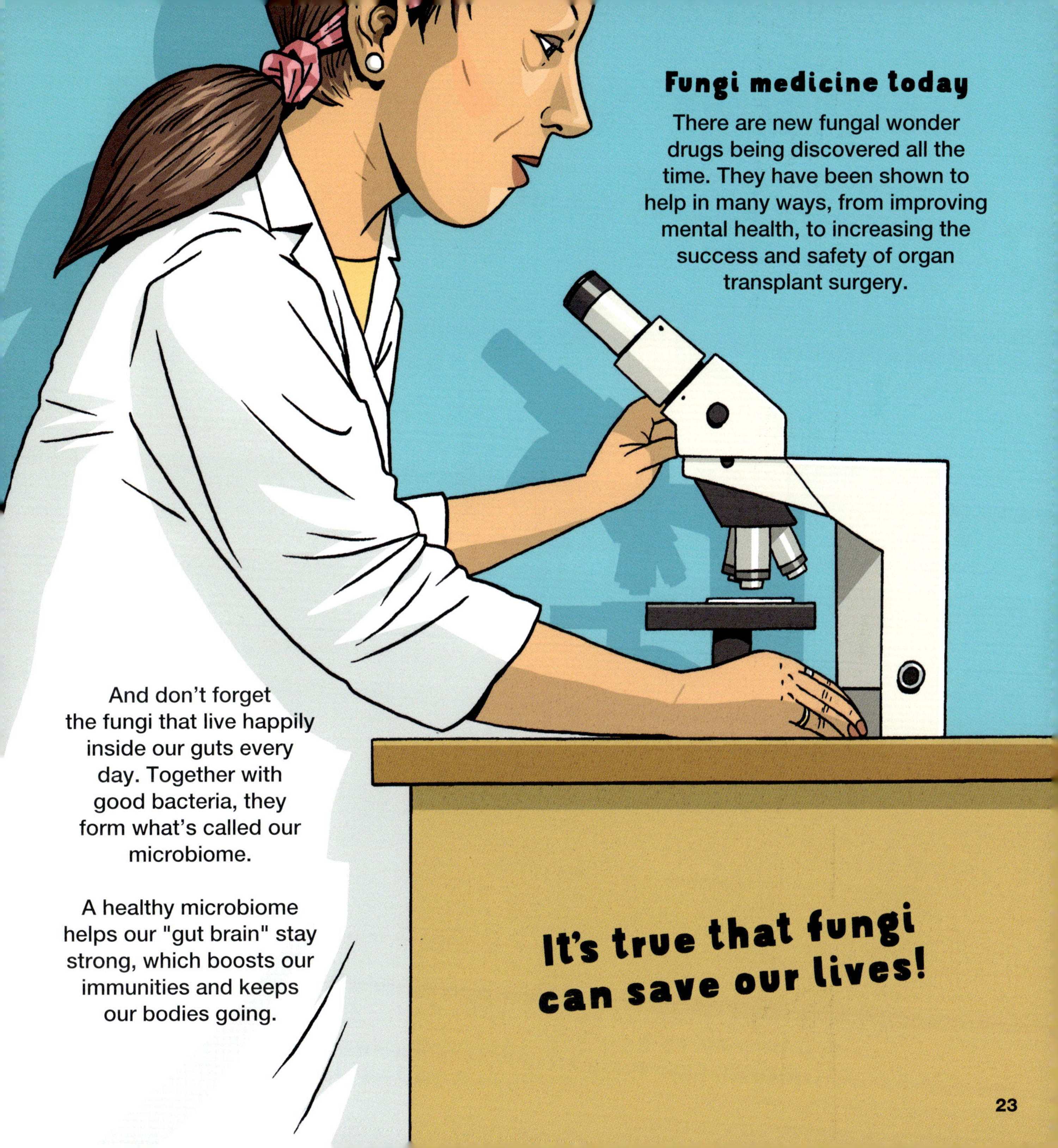

Fungi medicine today

There are new fungal wonder drugs being discovered all the time. They have been shown to help in many ways, from improving mental health, to increasing the success and safety of organ transplant surgery.

And don't forget the fungi that live happily inside our guts every day. Together with good bacteria, they form what's called our microbiome.

A healthy microbiome helps our "gut brain" stay strong, which boosts our immunities and keeps our bodies going.

It's true that fungi can save our lives!

Fungi as food and food for thought

The fruiting body of some fungi, called the mushroom, is tasty food for animals, from tiny, hairy fungus beetles to big bears and humans.

Mushroom meals

People who know a lot about fungi forage in their local areas for edible mushrooms, such as the chanterelle and the chestnut. There are more mushrooms in the wild than you will ever find in the average supermarket!

BUT DON'T TRY THIS. Some fungi are poisonous to humans, including the destroying angel, the funeral bell, and the deathcap.

Yeasts and molds

Some yeasts and molds are used in producing foods and drinks, including wine, beer, coffee, cheese, and even chocolate.

Yeasts and molds can also spoil food if they take over. Ever seen green fuzzy patches appearing on a piece of bread? That's a fungal mold and it means the bread is probably ready for the compost instead of the toaster.

The future of food

From meatless burgers to chickenless nuggets, tasty plant-based foods can be made from mycoprotein grown from the mycelium part of a fungus. It's cheap, delicious, and good for the planet and our bodies!

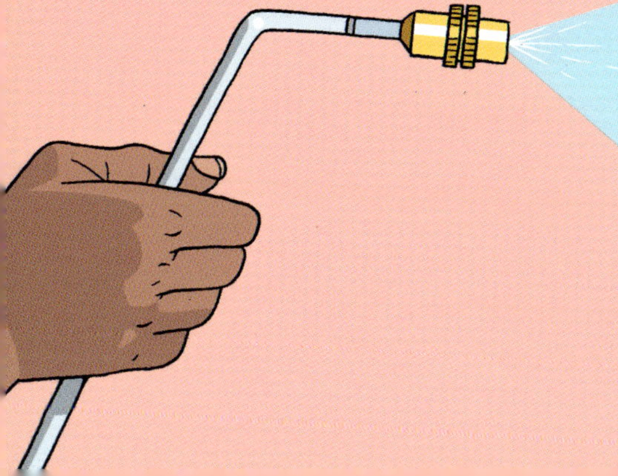

Fungi at risk, risks our world

Worldwide, farming with chemicals, such as fungicides, can upset the mycorrhizal network and make the soil less fertile and stable.

We need our worldwide mycorrhizal network to sustain our planet's food supply for all plants and animals.

Let's look to the future to see how fungi can help human beings protect our planet.

Fungi can

Fungi fights climate change

The mycorrhizal fungal networks also trap carbon. Too much carbon in Earth's atmosphere is a big contributor to global warming. Fungi help stop climate change!

Sustainable fungi

Fungi are being adapted into all kinds of useful and biodegradable materials.

Put that mushroom burger in a takeout container made from fungi! It's better for the planet than all that plastic packaging.

Fungi fashion could be the next big thing–who needs leather from animals when you have fungi leather?

Or what about growing a fungi building?

Mycelium makes strong bricks, so scientists are looking to make this the future of sustainable development.

save our world!

Fantastic fungi means beautiful biodiversity

We now know that many of our world's plants and animals depend on fungi to survive and thrive.

Where there are lots of fantastic fungi come lots of different plants and animals. Fungi help create this beautiful biodiversity for the future.

Fungi are amazing organisms! Let's all respect the work they do for the planet and for us.

What you can do for a fungus near you

About 150,000 species of fungi have been identified, but scientists estimate there are millions. Know your local fungi so you can educate your community.

Be a fungus detective

This chart depicts some of the most common fungi on all the continents of the world. Can you find some near you? Can you add to the list?

It's very important to *know* your fungi to *care* about them, but NEVER PICK MUSHROOMS OR LICHENS—leave that to the experts or simply leave them to grow.

KEY:
1. Fly agaric
2. Chanterelle
3. Horn of plenty
4. Shaggy parasol
5. Jelly ear
6. Common puffball
7. Common inkcap
8. Common earthstar
9. Scarlet elf cup
10. Oyster mushroom

Be a fungus artist

Make a spore print as a beautiful example of fungus power. You might also be able to identify the mushroom from the print if you're not sure what it is.

1. *With the help of an adult, get a mushroom (from a store is fine).*
2. *Remove the cap.*
3. *Place the cap down on a sheet of white paper (or dark paper if spores are white).*
4. *Cover it with a see-through cup or bowl and wait 6 to 12 hours.*

Spread the word

Finally, with permission, you could make a sign for your school or a local park, so that others know about all the life under their feet.

Fungi are everywhere and are vital to all life on Earth. They're on our bodies, in our food and in the ground we walk on. It's time to connect with fungi!

Glossary

Biodiversity – all the variety of life, whether that's plants, animals, fungi or micro-organisms, as well as the ecosystems they form and the habitats in which they live.

Carbon dioxide – a greenhouse gas used by plants, algae and some bacteria to make their own food through photosynthesis.

Decompose – to break down or decay. For example, some fungi decompose solid dead wood into tiny pieces that become part of a woodland floor.

Ecosystem – all the living organisms living in a certain area and how they interact with that environment.

Erosion – involves the movement of fragments of rock, soil, or sand by the action of wind, rain, or sun.

Fruiting body – the part of a fungus that produces spores.

Global warming – the process of our planet heating up and changes in our world weather. This is due to many reasons, including carbon dioxide escaping into the atmosphere.

Habitat – home environment for plants and animals or other organisms. Examples of habitats include: desert, meadow, woodland.

Microbes – the living microorganisms you cannot see with the naked eye, for example, tiny fungi, bacteria, and viruses.

Microbiome – the community of microorganisms (such as fungi, bacteria and viruses) that exists in a particular environment, such as our gut.

Mushroom – the fleshy, spore-bearing fruiting body of a fungus. It can be produced above ground, on soil, underground as in truffles, or on one of its food sources, such as a dead tree.

Mycologist – a scientist who works with and studies fungi.

Mycoprotein – a type of protein made from fungi for humans to eat.

Nutrients – any substance that plants, animals, or fungi need in order to live and grow.

Parasite – an organism benefitting from a living host, such as animals and humans.

Pollutant – any substance that makes the soil, water, or air dirty and unhealthy, such as radiation.

Sustainable development – how humans can interact with the environment in a way that ensures there will be enough resources left for future generations.

Symbiosis - when two different species live and interact together, such as fungi and plants.

Further info

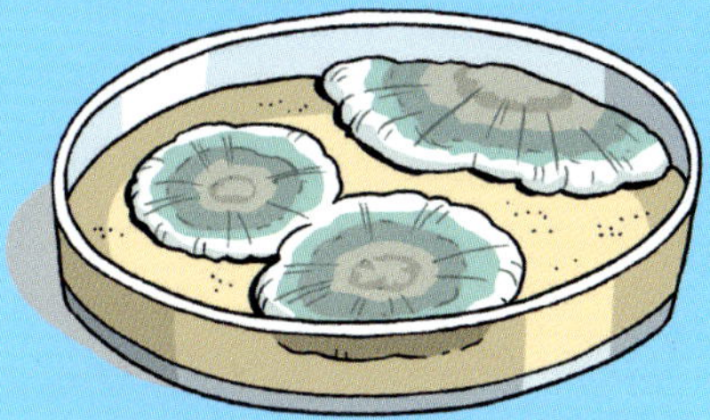

Find out more about the icky bits of nature!

Books:

An Anthology of Fungi
By Ali Ashby, et al., Dorling Kindersley Limited, 2024

The Bacteria Book
By Steve Mould, DK Publishing, 2024

Bugs Save the World
by Buglife, Wayland 2022

Plants Save the World
by Annabel Savery, Wayland 2022

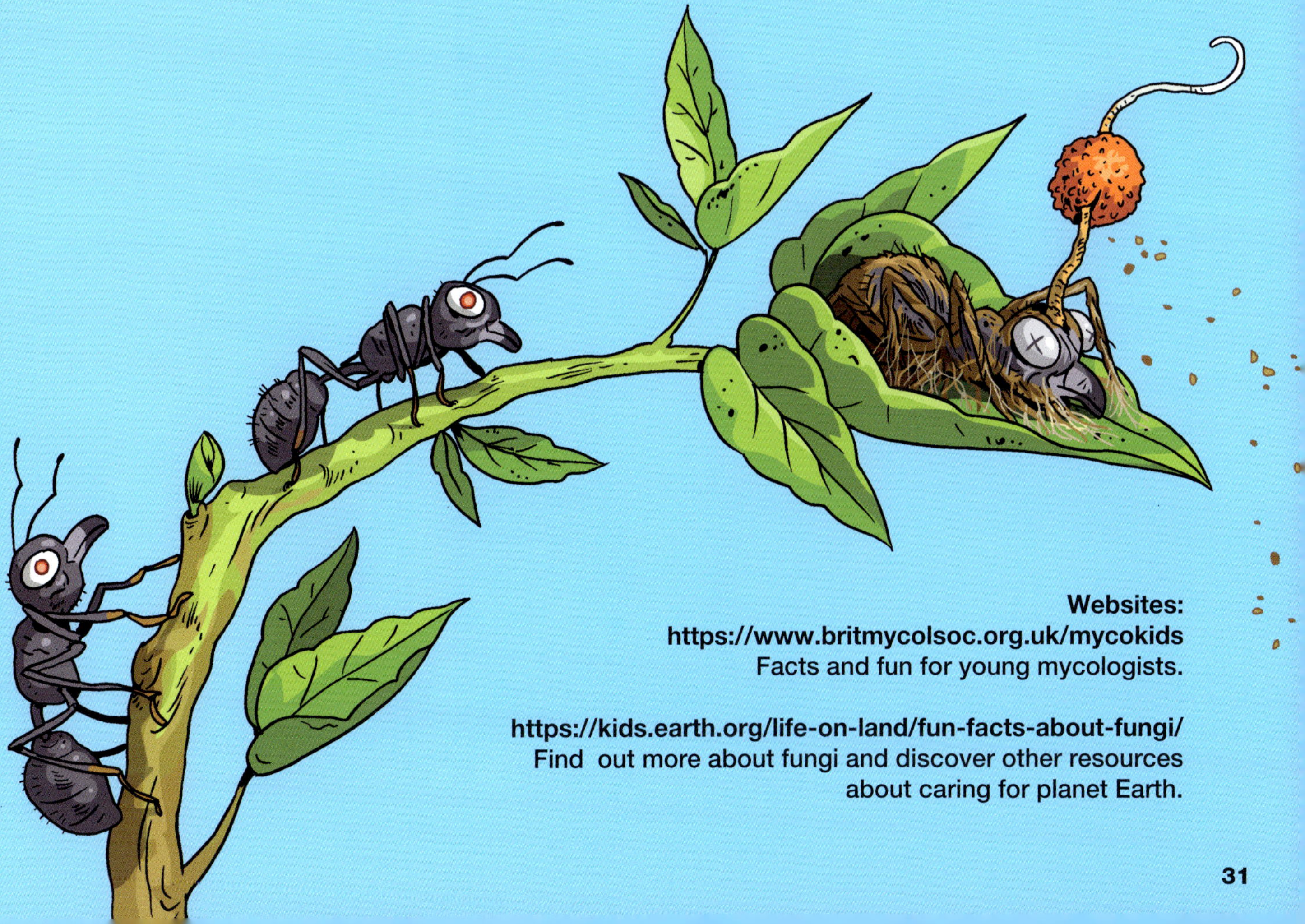

Websites:

https://www.britmycolsoc.org.uk/mycokids
Facts and fun for young mycologists.

https://kids.earth.org/life-on-land/fun-facts-about-fungi/
Find out more about fungi and discover other resources about caring for planet Earth.

INDEX

algae 6, 12
Antarctic 19
antibiotics 22
ants 10
Arctic 13
art 21, 29

bacteria 22, 23
biocrust 18
biodegradable 26
biodiversity 27
bioindicators 12
birds 13
bricks 26

camouflage 13
clothes 26
compost 11

decomposition 5, 11, 15
deserts 18
dinosaurs 7

erosion 18

fairies 20
first aid 23
Fleming, Alexander 22
food 5, 6, 8, 13, 24–25
forests
    boreal 13
    rainforests 10
    tropical 11
fungi
    athlete's foot 8
    baker's yeast
    black 19
    bracket 5, 22
    bread yeast 4
    caterpillar 22
    chanterelle 24, 28
    chestnut 24
    common earthstar 28
    common inkcap 28
    common puffball 28
    curtain crust 14
    deathcap 24
    destroying angel 24
    fly agaric 28
    funeral bell 24
    giant puffball 9
    honey 4
    horn of plenty 28
    human gut 8
    jelly ear 28
    microscopic 8, 18
    oyster mushroom 28
    parasitic 8, 15
    scarlet elf cup 28
    shaggy parasol 28
    stinkhorn 9
    white-rot 15
    zombie 11
fungicides 25
fungus gardens 11

global warming 13, 26
gut 8, 23

habitats 18
humans 8, 22, 26

immunities 23
insects 9, 10, 11
    flies 9
    termites 11
International Space Station 19

leaves 10, 14
lichens 4, 12–13, 21
lignin 15
logs 14

magic 20
medicines 5, 22, 23
microbiome 23
mildews 4
molds 4, 22, 25
mycelium 4, 7, 25
mycoprotein 25
mycorrhizal network 7, 16–17, 18, 25

nutrients 7, 8, 14, 16–17

organ transplant 23

packaging 26
penicillin 22
photosynthesis 16
plant rusts 4
plastics 18, 26
pollution 12, 18, 19
Potter, Beatrix 21

radiation 19
reindeer 13
roots 6, 7, 16

soil 16–17, 25
spores 9, 11, 29
stories 20
sustainable development 26
symbiosis 8

tardigrades 13

wood 14–15

yeasts 4, 25